T5-AFS-733

Bicycles

HISTORICAL TOYS

by Beth Dvergsten Stevens

Donated by
Michener P.T.O.

Perfection Learning® Corporation

Inside Illustration: Amy Sharp, Mike Aspengren, Kay Ewald

Dedication

For the avid bicyclists in my family and
for young riders everywhere. With special thanks
to my resident expert, Mike.

About the Author

Beth Stevens is a writer and former teacher. She currently writes stories and develops crafts and games for children's magazines. She also writes a weekly newspaper column for kids. Her first book, *Celebrate Christmas Around the World,* was a teacher's resource book.

Although she's no longer in the classroom, she still loves teaching and learning. She hopes her readers will discover something new and interesting every time they open one of her books! Beth lives in Waverly, Iowa, with her husband, three children, and their pets.

Image Credits: Art Today pp. 6, 7, 10, 11, 12 (top and middle), 16 (top), 17 (top), 28, 30 (inset), 35, 49, 50, 52; Corbis pp. 20, 23 (bottom), 26 (bottom); Corel pp. 14, 16 (bottom), 19 (top), 24, 31 (top and bottom), 33, 34 (top), 38, 53, 56; *The Des Moines Register* p. 27; Digital Stock p. 22; Eyewire p. 17 (bottom); Library of Congress pp. 13 (first, third); National Archives pp. 12 (bottom), 13 (second, fourth); PhotoDisc pp. 18, 19 (bottom), 21, 23 (top), 25, 26 (top), 31 (middle); Smithsonian pp. 4, 8, 29, 30

Text © 1999 by Perfection Learning® Corporation.
All rights reserved. No part of this book may be used or reproduced in any manner whatsoever without written permission from the publisher. Printed in the United States of America.
For information, contact
Perfection Learning® Corporation,
1000 North Second Avenue, P.O. Box 500,
Logan, Iowa 51546-1099.
Phone: 1-800-831-4190   Fax: 1-712-644-2392
Paperback ISBN 0-7891-2873-X
Cover Craft® ISBN 0-7807-7833-2

Table of Contents

CHAPTER

Historical Background of Bicycles

Would you like to ride a boneshaker? Or a hobbyhorse? How about a penny-farthing? These were the earliest bicycles. They were hard to ride. And the ride was very bumpy too!

The first bicycles were made of wood. They were very heavy.

These bicycles didn't have tires filled with air. And they didn't have soft seats. Some didn't even have pedals or handlebars! But people still thought they were wonderful.

People didn't have cars or trucks then. To go places, people walked or rode horses.

But people got tired. Their feet hurt. They couldn't travel very fast or far by walking.

Horses got tired too. They needed rest. They needed food. And they cost a lot of money.

People wanted to travel faster and easier. So inventors tried to think of other ways to travel.

In the late 1700s, a man in France thought of something. He watched children ride toy hobbyhorses.

An inventor is a person who thinks of something brand new and makes it for the first time.

People invent things to fix a problem. Or because they need something and can't find it.

I shall make one for grown-ups! he thought. And he did.

He built a big wooden horse on two wheels. He sat on the horse and pushed his feet along the ground. The hobbyhorse rolled.

This was faster than walking. He rode through a park. Everyone stared. Some people cheered. It was quite a show!

But the hobbyhorse had no pedals. It was heavy. The man couldn't ride it up hills. He couldn't steer it. And he couldn't even stop!

That didn't matter to young men in Paris. They thought hobbyhorses were fun! Soon many people rode them.

This invention made people think of better ones. Other inventors changed the hobbyhorse. They made it slimmer and lighter. It didn't look like a horse anymore. But it was still made of wood. And the driver still couldn't steer it.

Baron Karl von Drais
The Father
of the Bicycle

Baron von Drais worked in a forest. He had to walk many miles to work. His feet were sore! He wanted to get to his job faster. He invented a machine to help him. He invented the first true bicycle.

His bicycle was called a *Laufmaschine*, a *swift walker*, and a *draisienne* (draze-YEN). At first, people laughed at his invention. But later they were thankful for his great idea!

Then in 1816, a man in Germany had another idea. He added handlebars. He added a front wheel that turned. He could steer this bicycle!

He still had to use his feet. But when he was moving, he lifted them up. He balanced on two wheels! This bicycle rolled fast. In fact, some riders went as fast as a stagecoach! This was the first true bicycle.

Soon people everywhere wanted bicycles. Inventors in other countries copied the idea. They made the bicycles even better. They made them lighter. They made the seat softer.

These bicycles had different names.

Swift walkers, draisiennes, hobbyhorses, and dandy-horses.

But it was still hard work to ride them! Riders had to push with their feet along the ground. Their legs got tired. Soon people stopped buying these bicycles.

Inventors tried lots of things to make bicycles easy to ride. They tried levers and cranks. They tried three wheels. And four wheels. Some ideas were good. But most of these cycles were big and clumsy.

Then in 1839, a man in Scotland invented

Riding bicycles on city streets was dangerous. Dogs chased them. Horses became scared and ran wild. The streets were bumpy. And crowded.

People didn't know how to ride bicycles. So they went to riding schools to learn!

something great. Bicycle pedals! Riders pushed the pedals back and forth with their feet.

The pedals made the back wheel turn. A pedal bike was easier to ride! But the man never sold the idea. And people forgot about pedals for many years.

Finally, someone in France invented pedals again. They were on the front wheel. Riders pushed the pedals around with their feet. This  time, the pedals made the front wheel turn. This bicycle was called a *boneshaker.* People went crazy for it!

The wheels were made of wood. The tires were iron. And roads were very rough. A ride on a boneshaker bumped and rattled people's bones!

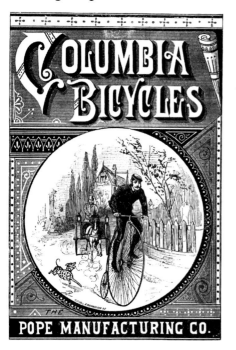

So inventors made more changes. They made metal frames. They put rubber on the wheels. And they made the front wheel very big. These bicycles were called *high wheelers, ordinaries,* or *penny-farthings.*

The big front wheel helped riders move fast. But on some bikes, the front wheel was too big! Some were five feet tall! Riders sat high

ALL STYLES & PRICES
THE AMERICAN CYCLES
DESCRIPTIVE CATALOGUE ON APPLICATION.
GORMULLY & JEFFERY MFG. CO. CHICAGO, ILL.
THE LARGEST MANUFACTURERS IN AMERICA

"AS YOU LIKE IT."
Installment Plan or CASH.
BICYCLES, TRICYCLES, VICTOR, VICTOR, JR., VICTOR SAFETY, SPALDING'S PREMIER. For full particulars address with stamp,
A.G. SPALDING & BROS.
108 Madison St., Chicago.
241 Broadway, New York.

in the air. They could not touch the ground.

It was hard to get on a high wheeler. A rider had to put one foot on a step. Then he pushed the bike forward and jumped

Why were some bikes called "penny-farthings"?

These bikes looked like two English coins lying next to each other. One coin was a large penny. The farthing was much smaller.

up to the seat! This took lots of practice.

A high wheeler was hard to ride too. If the front wheel hit a bump, the rider flew off! There were many crashes. And many injuries.

Daring young men could ride these bikes. But older men and women were afraid of them.

Did people give up on bicycles? No! They loved to ride. And they loved to travel. But they wanted bikes that were safe and easy for all riders.

So inventors added a wheel. They made fancy tricycles! Older people could ride these. Women

in long dresses could ride them too. Tricycles made for two people were called *sociables.*

And inventors made bicycles better too.

🚲 They added a chain and sprockets to turn the back wheel.

🚲 They made the front wheel smaller. The same size as the back wheel.

🚲 They changed the frame.

🚲 They moved the seat back.

And in 1888, John Dunlop made an important invention. A rubber tire filled with air. After that, bicycles were fast and smooth.

But stopping was very important! So inventors made better brakes.

This was called a *safety bicycle.* Everyone could ride it. Their feet touched the ground! It was very popular. The safety bicycle looked like bikes today.

But then something happened. The car was invented. Many adults quit riding bicycles.

Did bicycles die out? No! Children loved to ride them. So factories made smaller bikes for children.

Today, inventors are still thinking of changes. Bikes are very light. Brakes and tires are better. There are many gears to make riding easier. Bicycles are colorful and shiny. And some of them look very odd!

But one thing is the same. People of all ages still like to ride bicycles.

CHAPTER 2

Know Your Cycles

The Bicycle: Basic Parts

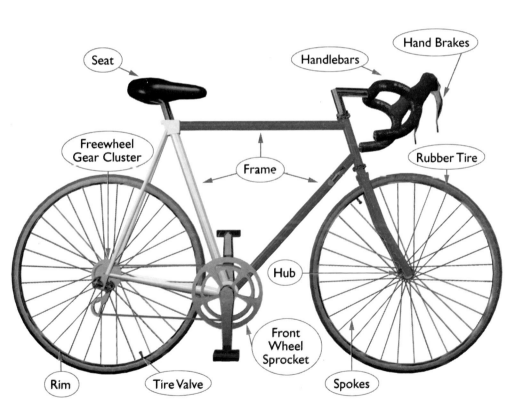

Kinds of Cycles

Inventors have made all kinds of cycles. The names can tell you about them. Look at these.

The names tell how many wheels a cycle has.

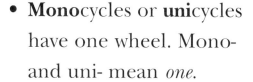

Brakes: Two Common Kinds

- Coaster Brakes: A rider pushes back on the pedal. The chain and back wheel stop moving.
- Hand Brakes: A rider squeezes levers on the handlebars. The levers pull a cable. The cable makes brakes grab the wheel rims, and the wheels stop moving.

- **Mono**cycles or **uni**cycles have one wheel. Mono- and uni- mean *one.*

- **Bi**cycles or **di**cycles have two wheels. Bi- and di- mean *two.*

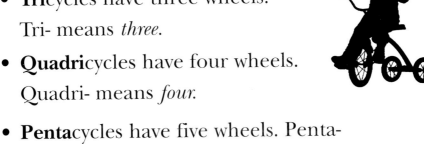

- **Tri**cycles have three wheels. Tri- means *three.*
- **Quadri**cycles have four wheels. Quadri- means *four.*
- **Penta**cycles have five wheels. Penta- means *five.*

These bicycle names tell how to use each one.

- **One-speed Bicycles** are good for beginners. There are no gears or different speeds. They usually have coaster brakes. The tires are fat and sturdy.

- **Touring Bicycles** are good for long rides. They are strong. Riders can carry packs on them. Tires can be thin or wide. Handlebars can turn down or be flat. They have many speeds. The seat should be comfortable!

- **Racing Bicycles** are made to go fast on roads or indoor tracks. These bikes are very light.

- **Road-Racing Bikes** have skinny tires. The handlebars turn down. They have many speeds.

- **Time-Trial Bikes** race on tracks. They look funny! The handlebars turn up like a cow's horns. They have disk wheels and sloping frames.

- **Mountain Bicycles** are made for off-road riding and bumpy ground. The tires are wide and knobby. The handlebars are straight across. There are lots of gears and speeds.

- **Hybrid Bicycles** are a cross between mountain and touring bikes. They have many gears, straight handlebars, and narrow tires.
- **Dirt Bicycles (BMX's)** have small frames and wheels. The handlebars are wide and tall. The tires are wide and knobby. They may have both kinds of brakes. The top tube is padded in case of falls.

- **Tandem Bicycles** have two wheels. One rider sits in back of the other rider. Each rider has a set of pedals. But only the driver can steer. Tandems can be built for two, three, or more!

- **Recumbents** are close to the ground. They are made for touring and commuting. Riders lean back on the seat. There are two or three wheels. The handlebars are by the knees. The pedals are in front of the rider.

How Are Cycles Used?

Bicycles are fun to ride. But they are used for other things too.

For Work

- **Police Officers:** Many police officers ride mountain bikes. They can chase criminals quickly. Police cars get stuck in traffic. They cannot go across yards or through narrow alleys. But bicycles can!

- **Bike Messengers:** In big cities, messengers ride bikes. They wear backpacks and carry two-way radios. They ride through traffic to deliver packages.
- **Delivery Riders:** People ride bicycles to deliver groceries, newspapers, tools, or mail.
- **Travelers:** There is a bicycle taxi service. In some cities, people ride in a special cart pushed or pulled by a bicycle. In Asia, this kind of bicycle is called a *trishaw.*

- **Merchants:** Shopkeepers use bicycles with a cart attached. They ride around. They sell flowers, ice cream, fruits, and vegetables from the cart.

For Commuting

Some people ride bicycles to work. It is good exercise. It is cheaper than a car. It saves gas. It is better for the environment.

These riders must be careful in traffic. And they may need to take a shower at work!

Famous Races

- RAAM (Race Across America): This is the longest nonstop bicycle race in the world. Riders go 3,100 miles without stopping much! They go through deserts, over mountains, and in rain. Riders sleep about three hours each night. Sometimes they fall asleep on their bicycles!

- Tour de France: This is the most famous bicycle race in the world. Riders travel 2,000 to 3,000 miles in 23 stages. The leader after each stage gets to wear a yellow shirt. There are lots of steep mountain roads. Greg LeMond was the first American to win this race.

- Triathalons: There are races with bicycling, swimming, and running. Racers swim first. Then they bike 25 miles and run 6 miles. The first Hawaii Ironman Triathalon was held in 1976. Ironman racers go even farther!

For Racing

Some riders race for fun. Others race to make money! It is their job.

There are indoor races on special tracks. There are outdoor races on roads. Each race uses a different kind of bicycle.

Racers must exercise and train a lot. They must eat good foods. And they must drink a lot of water!

25

For Recreation

Everyone can go bicycling. Older people might like adult tricycles. Other people enjoy tandem bikes.

Little children can ride in child seats or bike trailers. Some families form a bicycle train.

Bike trails are safer than streets. There are no cars or trucks. Many old railroad tracks are being turned into bike trails. It's also fun to ride on smooth trails.

Some states plan special rides across their states. One of the oldest rides takes place in Iowa. It's called *RAGBRAI* (**R**egister's **A**nnual **G**reat **B**icycle **R**ide **A**cross **I**owa). It takes seven days to ride across Iowa. Riders go 50 to 100 miles each day. Thousands of people from all over the world come to Iowa each July to ride on **RAGBRAI.**

Photo by Tina Yee, Copyright 1998, The Des Moines Register and Tribune Company. Reprinted with permission.

CHAPTER 4

Strange Bicycles

Bicycles are amazing inventions. Look at these odd ones.

From the Old Days

- **Tandem Safety:** An ordinary for two people. The rider in the back steered the rear wheel.

- **Dicycle:** The rider sat between two big wheels. The wheels were side by side. To steer, the rider turned one wheel faster than the other one.

- **Swing Bicycle:** Two riders sat in a basket between two huge wheels. They pulled levers to make the basket swing. This made the bike move.
- **Monocycle:** Riders sat or stood inside one huge wheel and pedaled.
- **Big-Wheel Unicycle:** The rider sat on top of one huge wheel.

- **Sociable:** Two riders sat next to each other on this tricycle. Sweethearts liked these!

- **Coventry Tricycle:** A big wheel on one side with two smaller wheels on the other side. The rider sat in the middle.

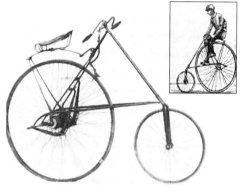

- **American Star:** It looked like an ordinary with the seat turned around! The big wheel was in the back.

- **French Giraffe:** This very tall bicycle was used in circus acts.

- **Rail Bike:** This bicycle rolled on a railroad track. Look out for trains!

From Modern Times

- **Carnival Bike:** People invent strange bicycles for contests! The longest bike. The most tires. The most chains. Recycled bicycles. Water bicycles. Sand bicycles. They are fun to see!

- **Exercise Bicycle:** People pedal this bike indoors for exercise. You can't go anyplace though!

- **Folding Bicycle:** These bicycles fold up and fit into a case. They aren't very heavy to carry.

- **The Speedy:** This fast bike has three wheels. It sits close to the ground. The rider leans back and pedals in front.

Bikes of the Future?

- **Kingcycle:** A small recumbent bicycle that is very fast.
- **The Bean:** Is it a car? Is it a bicycle? It is really a covered racing bike. A rider can go up to 65 miles per hour!
- **The Ecocar:** Pedal power makes this bicycle-car go.

CHAPTER 5

How to Bicycle Safely

Warm-Up Exercises

Warm up your muscles before a big ride. Then you won't get sore and tired.

1. Do ten toe touches.

2. Stand two feet away from a wall. Step forward with one foot. Put your hands on the wall and lean toward it. Do you feel your back leg stretch? Hold the position. Count to 20. Do it with the other leg.

3. Stand on one leg. Grab your other ankle and pull it up. Count to 15. Don't fall over! Do it with your other ankle.

4. Do five sit-ups.

5. Get down on your hands and knees. Stretch your head down. Then lift your head up. Do this ten times.

The Right Equipment

1. Be sure your bicycle fits you.

    a. Sit on the seat. Your feet should touch the ground.

    b. When your foot is on the low pedal, your leg should be almost straight.

    c. Can you reach the hand brakes?

    d. Move the seat up or down so the bike fits you just right.

2. Have the right gear.
   a. Always wear a good helmet!
   b. Use a bright headlight. Use flashing rear lights. These lights make you easier to see. Turn on your lights when it starts to get dark.
   c. Put reflectors on your wheels and pedals.
   d. Carry a water bottle. Drink lots of water on long rides.
   e. Use a chain and lock to keep your bicycle safc.
   f. A tire pump is a good tool. Know how to use it.
   g. Bells or horns warn others you are nearby.

Choose the Right Bicycle

Ages	Wheel size
2–3 years old	12-inch wheels on tricycle or bike with training wheels
4–6 years old	16-inch wheels on small BMX style bike
7–11 years old	20-inch wheels on children's bike, any style
12 years and older	24- or 26-inch wheels on small adult frame

The Rules of the Road

Take This Quiz!
Write your answers on a separate sheet of paper.
Answers on pages 54–56.

1. Always wear a _____.

2. Ride on the _____
   side of the road.

3. Ride (with or against) the car traffic.

4. Do you have to stop at stop signs?

   _____

5. Obey all bicycle _____
   in your town.

6. Look _____
   ways before crossing a street.

7. To make a right-hand turn, _____

   _____

   _____.

8. To make a left-hand turn, _____ _____ _____.

9. The best time to ride is _____ _____.

10. If your friend asks to ride on your bike with you, say _____ _____.

11. What are some things you should watch out for when you ride your bike?

12. List some important equipment you should have.

And please don't ride on busy streets alone!

Sharpen Your Bicycling Skills

Try these games to become a better rider!

1. Set up plastic cones or empty coffee cans in a big zigzag line. Ride your bicycle around them. Did you knock any down?

2. Draw a long, straight chalk line. Ride your bicycle on the line. Could you stay on it?

3. Draw a start and finish line on the sidewalk. Ride your bicycle as **slowly** as you can. Ask a friend to time you. How long did it take to reach the finish line? Now ride it **fast!** Practice braking. Could you stop quickly?

CHAPTER **6**

Make It!
Bicycle Accessories

How can you carry things on a bike? In packs. Carry things to keep you safe. Like a name tag and first aid kit. Follow these directions to make your own gear!

Bike Pack

Needs

- 1 leg from old sweat pants or blue jeans with a hole in the knee

- ruler

- pencil

- scissors

- straight pins

- needle and thread

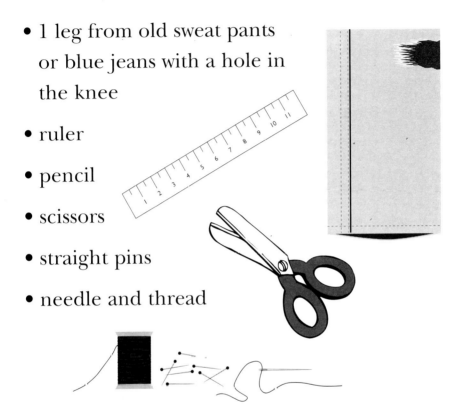

For strap pack: 10 inches of strapping, 3-inch strip of sticky Velcro®

For drawstring pack: 2 shoelaces or 2 pieces of cord (Each piece should be about 24 inches long.)

Optional: puffy paints, patches

Steps

1. Cut off elastic or hem at bottom of the pants leg.

2. Measure 12 inches up from cut. Draw a line across the pant leg. Cut along line. Now you have a tube of fabric. Turn it inside out.

3. Fold widest cut edge up to make a hem about 1 inch wide. Pin in place.

4. Sew around hem close to cut edges. Or ask an adult to help you use the sewing machine.

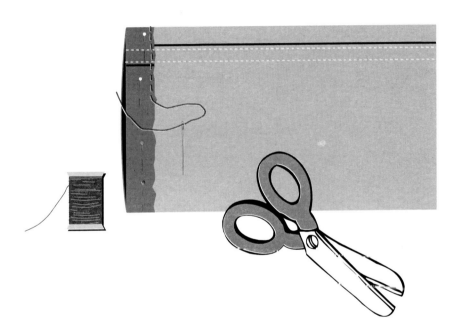

For Strap Pack

5. Flatten tube with seams at side edges. Sew bottom edge together.

6. Turn right side out.

7. Cut strapping in half. Each piece will be 5 inches long.

8. Decorate pack with paints or patches.

9. Sew or glue one end of each strap to back inside edge at the top of pack, one near each seam.

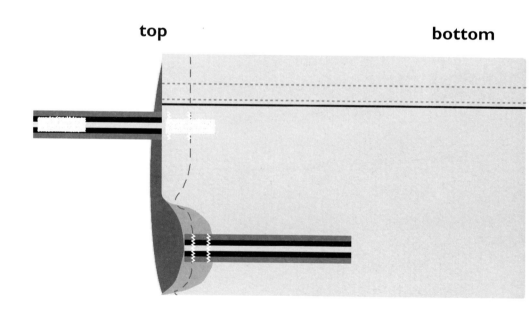

top   **bottom**

10. Cut Velcro in half. Each piece will be 1½ inches long. Attach a stiff piece of Velcro to each strap end on back side.

11. Attach the fuzzy pieces of Velcro to top edge of pack on outside as shown.

12. Fill pack. Wrap straps over handlebars. Press Velcro together to hold in place.

Check your hand brakes. Be sure they still work with the pack on!

For Drawstring Pack

Complete steps 1 through 4.

5. Hem other cut edge the same way.

6. Cut a small hole on each side of the hem at both ends.

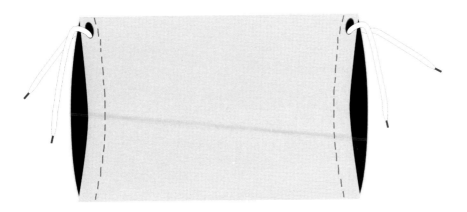

7. Thread shoelaces into holes and through both hems.

8. Decorate pack with paints or patches.

9. Fill pack. Pull laces to close pack. Tie onto handlebars or cross bar. To get your gear out, untie one end and open pack.

Bicycler's Name Tag Necklace (ID tag)

Needs

- typing paper

- scissors

- poster board

- pen

- glue

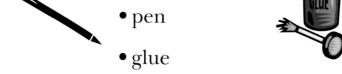

- clear contact paper

- paper punch

- 30 inches of yarn or shoelace

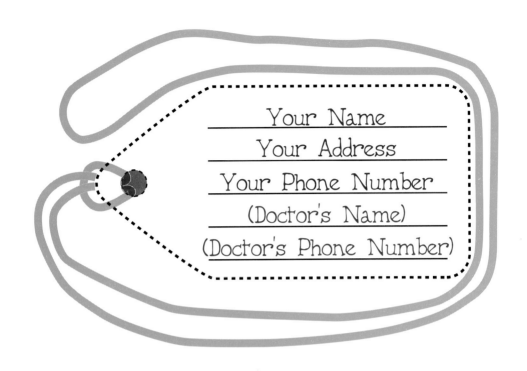

Your Name
Your Address
Your Phone Number
(Doctor's Name)
(Doctor's Phone Number)

Steps

1. Trace this pattern onto typing paper. Cut it out.

2. Trace around your pattern on poster board two times. Cut out both shapes.

3. Glue the two shapes together.

4. On one side, carefully print your name, address, and phone number. Add your doctor's name and number too. Include any allergies you have.

5. Cover with contact paper. Trim.

6. Punch a hole in the small end. Thread tag onto yarn or shoelace. Tie ends.

Wear this necklace every time you go bicycling!

First Aid Kit

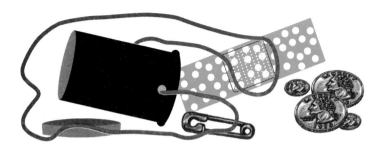

Needs

- paper punch
- plastic film or spice container (with lid)
- 30 inches of yarn or shoelace
- Band-Aid®
- 2 quarters and 2 dimes
- safety pin
- antiseptic wipe
- cotton ball

Steps

1. Make 2 holes at top edges of container.

2. Put yarn or shoelace through holes to
   the inside. Tie a knot at each end.

3. Fill container with first aid items.

Wear this around your neck on a bicycle
ride. Or put it into your pack. Use the coins
for a phone call if you need help!

CHAPTER 7

Think About It! Cycle Trivia

🚲 Why did early bicycle riders wear out their shoes quickly? Bicycles didn't have brakes! Riders dragged their feet to stop.

🚲 Why were blacksmiths mad when bicycles were invented? People rode bicycles instead of horses. And bicycles didn't need horseshoes. Blacksmiths lost a lot of work.

🚲 Why was the first bicycle with rubber tires called a *Phantom*? This bicycle was so quiet. Like a phantom! Bikes with metal tires were much noisier.

🚲 Bicycles hurt some businesses because

- bicycle riders didn't buy hats anymore. Hats would fly off their heads.

- bicycle riders didn't buy nice suits. Clothes tore easily on bike rides.

- bicycle riders stopped going to theaters. They stayed home to save their money. For bicycles!

🚲 Ordinaries had very big front wheels. Riders needed long legs to reach the pedals. One smart man made his legs longer. He wore shoes with very thick soles!

🚲 In Japan and China, many people ride bicycles to work.

🚲 When a man got married in China, he had to buy three things for his wife. All three things must "go around"—a watch, a sewing machine, and a bicycle.

Crazy Bicycle Stunts and Tricks

- Some riders have bicycle races under water!
- Some riders jump their bikes over things.
- There are sky-diving bicyclists with parachutes.
- A record: 19 people on a one-seat bicycle!
- One rider popped a wheelie for about 1 hour and 17 minutes.
- Some riders do freestyle cycling. They go up and down ramps. Then they fly into the air and do stunts. Helicopter and Windshield Wiper are two of the stunts.

🚲 Some people have bicycle weddings. Guests throw ball bearings instead of rice!

🚲 What does *faceplant* mean? For bicyclists, it means falling off your bike head first!

🚲 The Eiffel Tower in France has 1,710 steps. One man rode his bicycle from the top to the bottom. A bumpy ride!

🚲 There are 800 million bicycles in the world.

🚲 Racing teams work together to ride faster. How? They draft. Drafting is when the racers ride in a line. Their wheels almost touch! The first rider works the hardest. He breaks the wind for the other riders.

When the leader gets tired, he gives a signal. He moves to the end of the line. The next rider moves to the front. Every rider takes a turn leading. The other riders draft behind. It takes a lot of practice. If one racer goofs, all of them may crash!

Would you like to ride a bike without brakes? Track racers do! The track is flat. They ride as fast as they can. They may ride 50 miles per hour. When the race is over, they pedal slowly until they stop.

🚲 How long can you balance on your bike without moving? One man in Japan did it for almost 5½ hours!

🚲 *Cyclo-cross* racing is very hard. Bicycle riders go over snow, across rivers, or through forests. Sometimes riders have to carry their bikes!

🚲 Some bicycles are driven with hands. People who cannot use their legs can ride these.

The Rules of the Road

Answers

1. Always wear a _____**helmet**_____.

2. Ride on the _____**right**_____ side of the road.

3. Ride (_____**with** or against_____) the car traffic.

4. Do you have to stop at stop signs? _____**yes**_____

5. Obey all bicycle _____**laws**_____ in your town.

6. Look _____**both**_____ ways before crossing a street.

7. To make a right-hand turn, **stay to the far right side of the road. Slow down. Make the hand signal for a right turn. Make a careful turn. Stay in the right-hand lane of the street.**

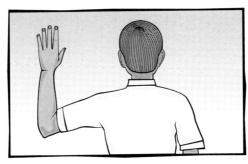

8. To make a left-hand turn, **slow down. Make the hand signal for a left turn. Look in back and in front for cars. Turn only if it is safe. If there is too much traffic, stop at the curb. Get off your bike. Wait until it is safe. Then push your bike across the street.**

9. The best time to ride is _____**daytime**_____.

10. If your friend asks to ride on your bike with you,

    say _____**no**_____.

11. What are some things you should watch out for when you ride your bike? Possible answers include **holes in the road, dogs, cars, broken glass, sand, sharp rocks, walkers, wet leaves,** and so on.

12. List some important equipment you should have. Possible answers include **helmet, reflective tape on clothing, rearview mirror, water bottle, first aid kit, tire-patch kit,** and so on.